THROUGH THEIR EYES

A Collection of Student Voices, Memories, and Appreciation

By

Horatio Ward

Published by

Ward Publishing

Fort Myers, Florida

Through Their Eyes

Published by:

Ward Publishing

Fort Myers, Florida, USA

Ward Publishing: https://wardpublishing.org

ISBN: **979-8-9963893-0-8**

First Edition

Cover design by Ward Publishing

Disclaimer

Every reasonable effort has been made to protect the identities and privacy of the children featured in this book. In some instances, names, identifying details, photographs, or personal information may have been changed, abbreviated, omitted, cropped, blurred, or used with permission in order to safeguard student confidentiality and well-being.

The messages, letters, notes, drawings, and written expressions included in this collection are presented authentically and exactly as they were originally created by the students. No edits or corrections have been made to spelling, grammar, punctuation, wording, or artistic expression, except where necessary to remove or obscure identifying information.

This collection is intended solely to celebrate the positive impact of education, mentorship, and the meaningful connections formed within the school community. The thoughts and expressions shared herein are included with gratitude, care, and deep respect for the students and families who inspired them.

Dedication

This book is dedicated to every student who ever walked into my classroom carrying dreams, struggles, questions, laughter, and hope.

Thank you for allowing me to be part of your journey.

Your words, your growth, and your resilience have inspired me far more than you may ever realize.

Teaching was never just about lessons and grades.

It was about connection.

It was about belief.

It was about seeing one another.

And through your eyes, I discovered the true meaning of education.

Horatio Ward

Acknowledgments

To my students — past and present — thank you for the memories, the laughter, the challenges, and the countless moments that made every school year meaningful.

To the families who trusted me with their children, thank you for your support and encouragement.

To my colleagues, mentors, and friends who continue to uplift and inspire educators every day, your dedication never goes unnoticed.

And to my family, thank you for your unwavering love, patience, and belief in me throughout this journey.

This book exists because of the people whose lives touched mine inside and outside the classroom.

Preface

There are moments in teaching that never appear on lesson plans, pacing guides, or standardized tests.

Moments when a student quietly says, "Thank you."

Moments when a handwritten note appears on your desk after a difficult day.

Moments when former students return years later simply to say, "You made a difference."

Those moments matter.

Through Their Eyes was born from the realization that the greatest measure of an educator's impact is not found in data charts or evaluation scores, but in the hearts and memories of the students whose lives we touch.

Within these pages are words of appreciation, reflections, photographs, memories, and glimpses into the relationships built inside a classroom community. Some messages are humorous. Some are emotional. Some are short and simple. Yet each one represents something deeply meaningful: connection.

Teaching is often exhausting work. It demands patience, sacrifice, resilience, and heart. But every now and then, students remind us why we started.

This book is not just my story.

It is theirs.

And through their eyes, I hope readers will see the beauty, humanity, and lasting power of education.

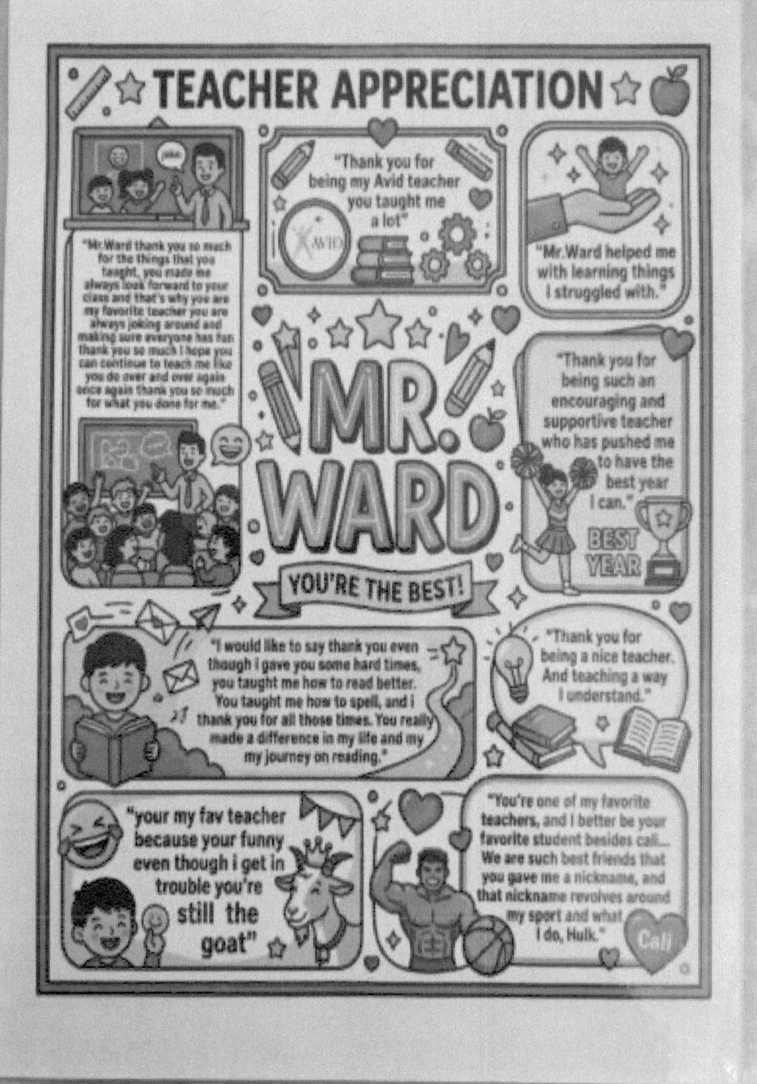
TEACHER APPRECIATION
"Thank you for being my Avid teacher you taught me a lot"
AVID
"Mr.Ward helped me with learning things I struggled with."
"Mr.Ward thank you so much for the things that you taught, you made me always look forward to your class and that's why you are my favorite teacher you are always joking around and making sure everyone has fun thank you so much I hope you can continue to teach me like you do over and over again once again thank you so much for what you done for me."
MR. WARD
YOU'RE THE BEST!
"Thank you for being such an encouraging and supportive teacher who has pushed me to have the best year I can."
BEST YEAR
"I would like to say thank you even though I gave you some hard times, you taught me how to read better. You taught me how to spell, and I thank you for all those times. You really made a difference in my life and my my journey on reading."
"Thank you for being a nice teacher. And teaching a way I understand."
"your my fav teacher because your funny even though i get in trouble you're still the goat"
"You're one of my favorite teachers, and I better be your favorite student besides cali... We are such best friends that you gave me a nickname, and that nickname revolves around my sport and what I do, Hulk."
Cali

Dear Mr. Ward
Thank you for leading me into a good Path. You helped me with work with Problems. One thing i appreciate most about you is you are funny you are the only Person that can make me laugh. because of you i feel happy and welcome. You are my second favorit teacher. You make our classroom a better Place because you make us feel loved. Thank you so much

it been going All
right I try helping someone
and they are so rude
it happened today so
well when I messed something
I try helping they say I
dont care I try helping
again and one of them say
shut up I found that
very rude and people in this
school are very rude
only reason my school
hasn't been bad is Mr. ward
How Funny He is and kind
and my Friends if For
them I would have move out
the school so yeah my school
been allrigth Just people so
rude and Mrs. Haverton was
pretty Nice and only reason
she gets mad because
people act up and been
rude to her thanks For
reading How my school year
been

We the following
HEREBY
ADOPT
Mr. Ward
AS OUR
SCHOOL DAD
THANK YOU FOR BEING AWESOME!
YOU MAKE OUR SCHOOL A BETTER PLACE!
We promise to: Work hard Be kind Show respect Encourage others Make you proud
1
2
3
4
5
Thank you for being more than just a teacher.
You guide us, support us, make us laugh, and believe in us.
We're lucky to have you as our School Dad!

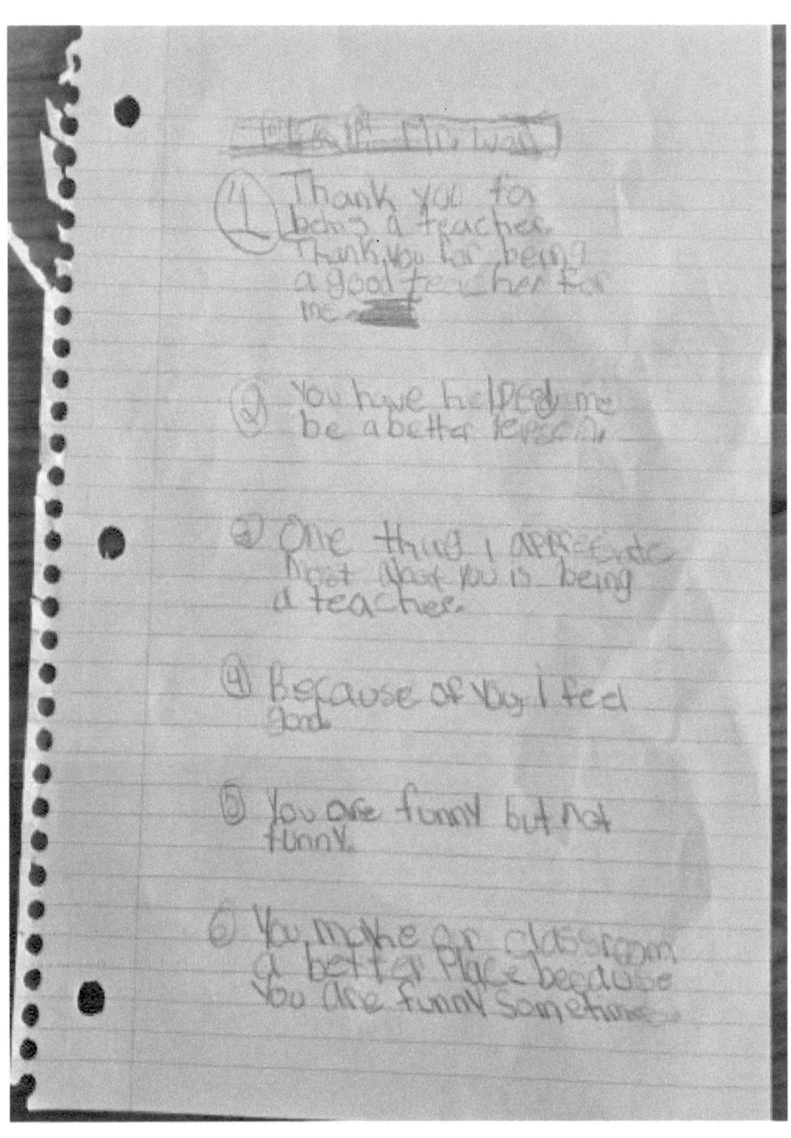

1. Thank you for being a teacher. Thank you for being a good teacher for me.
2. You have helped me be a better person.
3. One thing I appreciate most about you is being a teacher.
4. Because of you I feel good.
5. You are funny but not funny.
6. You make our classroom a better place because you are funny sometimes.

P.4 5/13/26

Dear Mr. ward thank you for making my first
days here easy. You have helped me in ways other
teachers can't even if you didn't know.
One thing I appreciate about you is how
even though you're struggling you're still the best
version of yourself for your students.
Because of you, I feel motivated and confident
in my work and future. You are a good person
in my opinion because you're a paticent and
cheerful person. You make our classroom a better
place because you're always making people laugh without
even trying, and everyone feels comfortable enough
to talk to you and go to you when they're feeling
down. I am proud to call you my favorite teacher.

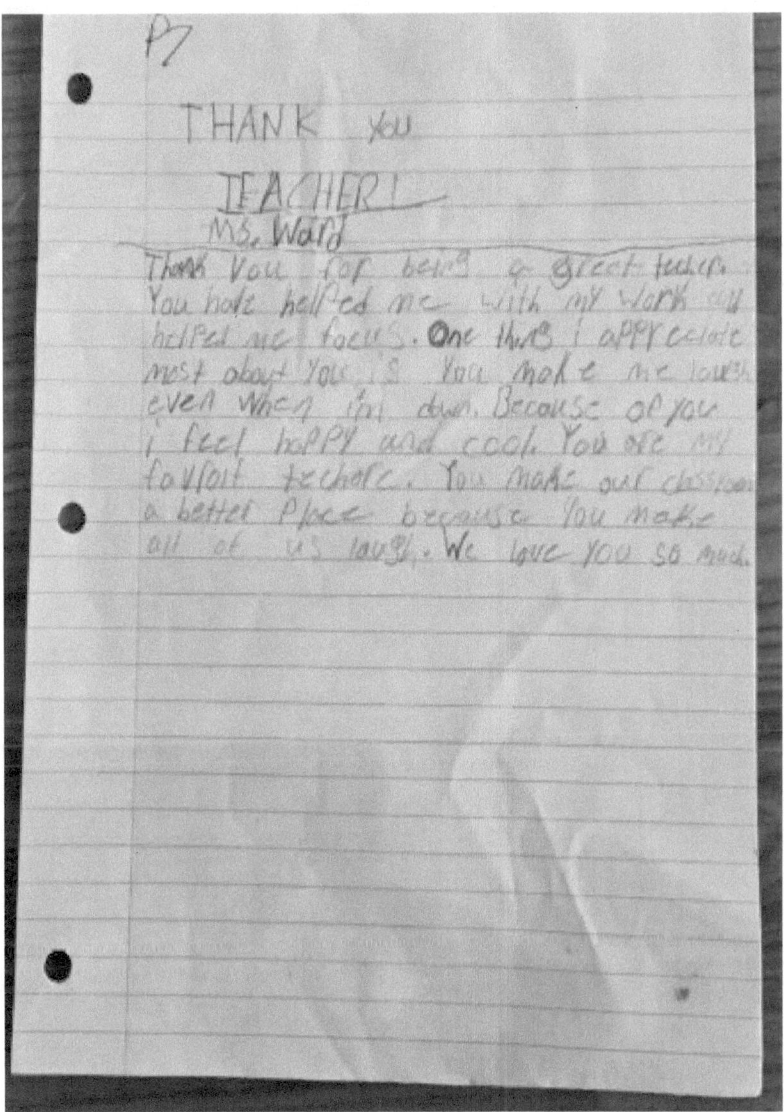

THANK you

TEACHER!

Ms. Ward

Thank You for being a great techer. You have helped me with my Work and helped me focus. One thing i appreciate most about You is You make me laugh even when i'm down. Because of you i feel happy and cool. You are my favorit techere. You make our classroom a better Place because You make all of us laugh. We love You so much.

HAPPY Birthday

MR. Ward!!!!

Dear, Mr. Ward, I hope you have a really good birthday and a really good day, thank you for being such a good teacher, your really nice, funny, and cool, im glad to have you as a teacher. may your wishes come true on this very magical day for you!!!

PS. don't forget me next year im in your 6th period! :)

Happy Birthday!
Mr
Ward
AVID

Thank you Mr Ward for cheering me up when I'm down and giving me a chance to change. You
have helped me by teaching me the ways of avid. One thing i appreciate most about you is how you make everything funny. Because of you i feel accepted, you are one of the greatest teachers i know. You make our class a better place because we have learned to make everyone welcome.

Thank You
Your act of kindness was the perfect gesture, and I want to convey my deepest appreciation. Thank you for making a difference in my life
Mr Ward

From: 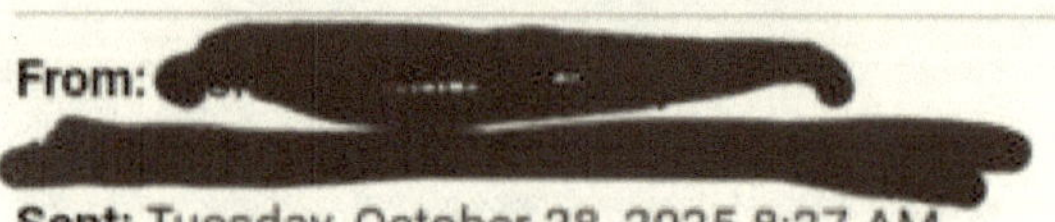

Sent: Tuesday, October 28, 2025 8:27 AM
To: Ward, Horatio <horatiow@LeeSchools.net>
Subject: Thank you

Good morning, Mr.Ward

I hope this email finds you well. I wanted to thank you for being one of my favorite teachers. Even though you only taught me for one year, you made the best out of it. Thank you for teaching me many life lessons and keeping me on track. You helped me get better at school and also helped me become a better and smarter person.

Additionally, I wanted to share my high school experiences with you thus far, the first quarter just passed and I think I did pretty good. But I know I can do better. I've made many new friends and I'm starting to like this school. I still have avid and still good with trf because you taught us how to do them.

With great appreciation,

Thank you
MR.WARD
Thank you for helping me out when
I was struggling in different classes

THANK YOU MR. WARD!

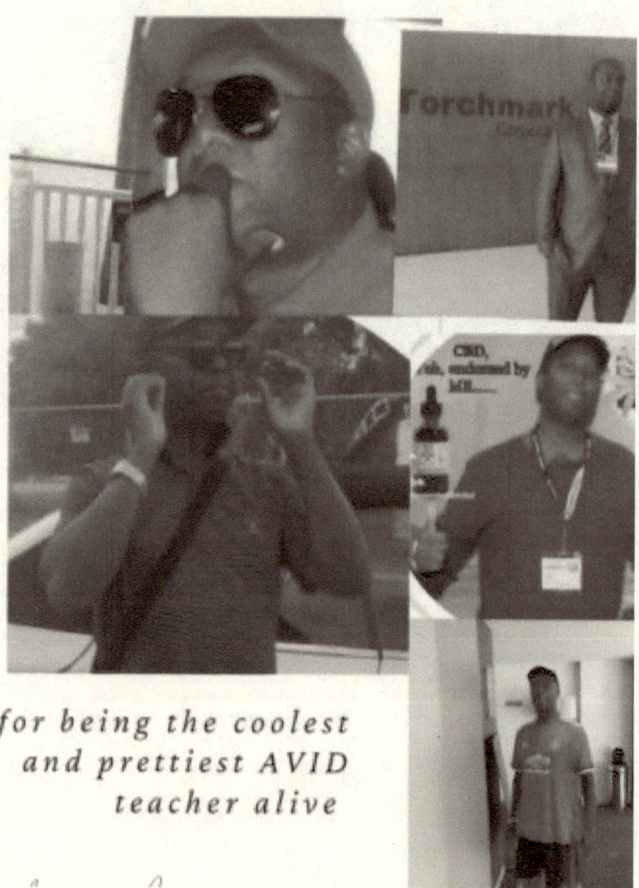

for being the coolest and prettiest AVID teacher alive

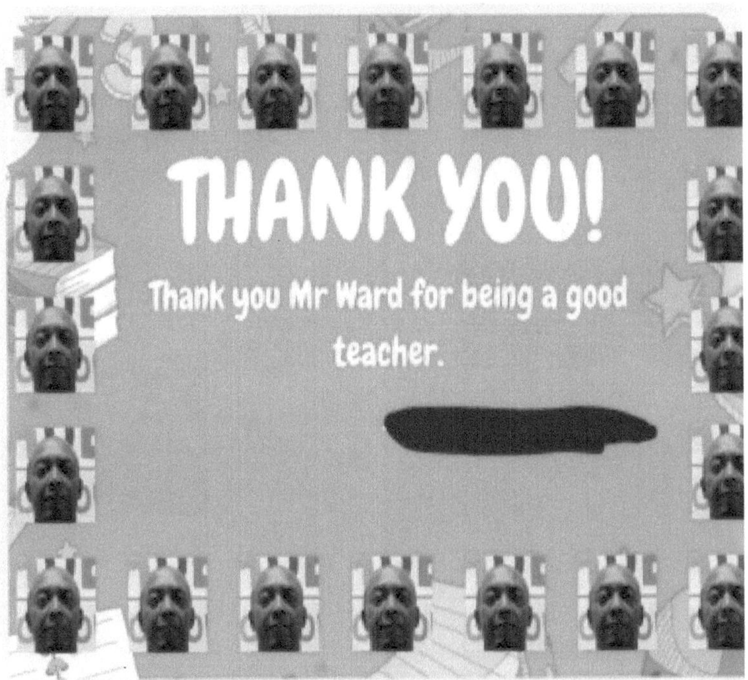
THANK YOU!
Thank you Mr Ward for being a good teacher.

thank you
mr.ward
"A teacher can inspire hope , ignite the imagination and instill a love of learning"
KitKat
From:A
To:Mr.ward

THANK YOU MR.WARD
YOU ARE MY FAVORITE AND WONDERFUL TEACHER I COULD EVER ASK FOR.

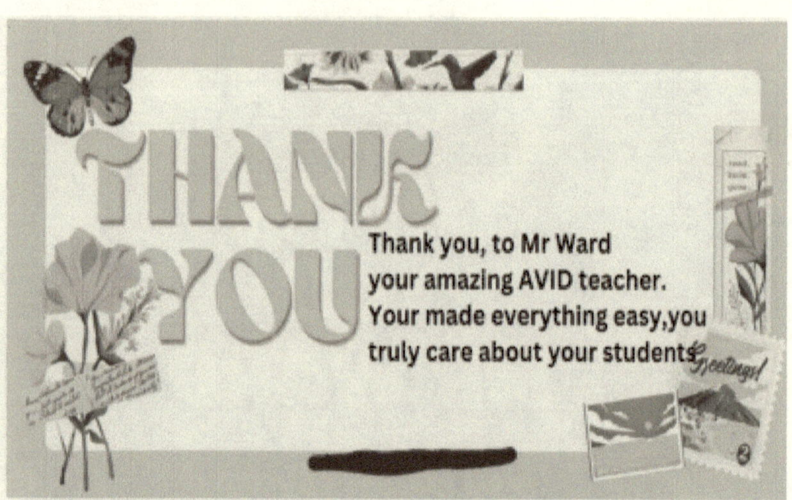
THANK
YOU
Thank you, to Mr Ward
your amazing AVID teacher.
Your made everything easy,you
truly care about your students
Greetings!

Thank you!
Mr. Ward
for being a great
avid teacher
AVID

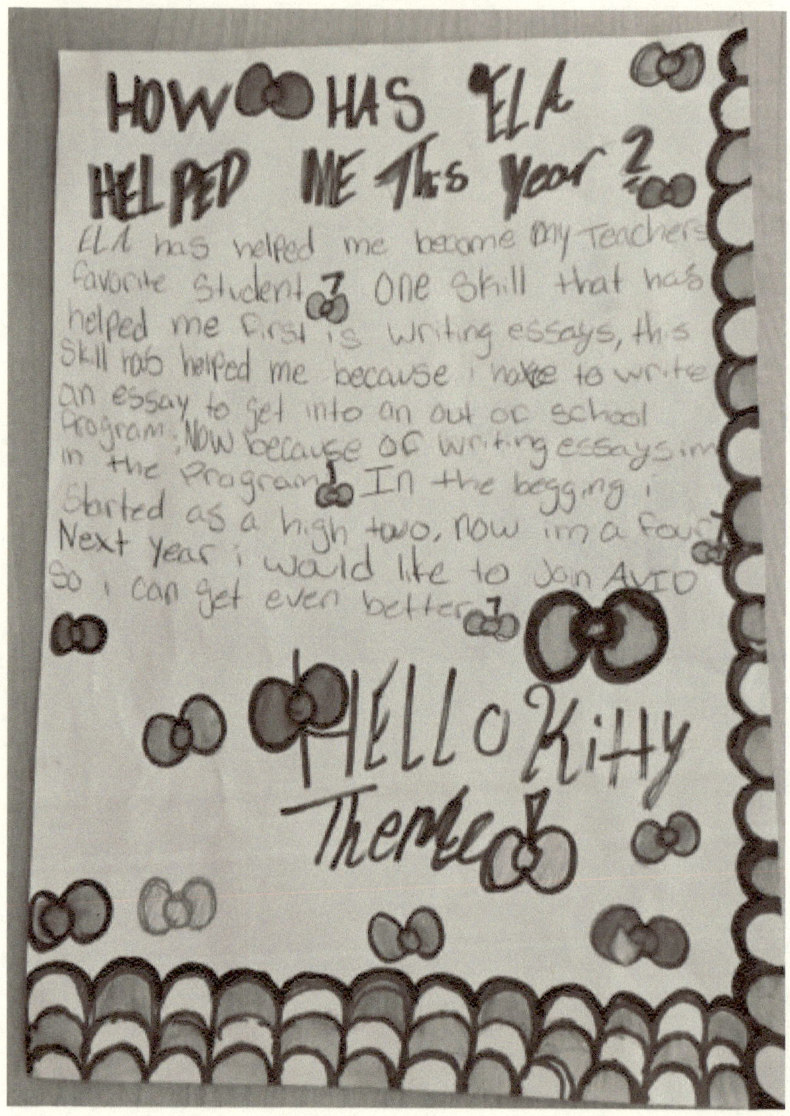
HOW HAS ELA
HELPED ME This Year?
ELA has helped me become my Teachers
favorite Student. One skill that has
helped me first is writing essays, this
skill has helped me because i have to write
an essay to get into an out of school
Program. Now because of writing essays im
in the Program. In the begging i
started as a high two, now im a four.
Next Year i would like to join AVID
so i can get even better.
HELLO Kitty
Theme!

Peace
You get me?
I have eyes in the back of my head
Thing Mr. Ward Says:
Yeah man!
Why you looking the other way?
Ziggy!
Pacey
can you see me?
Nathaniel I told you don't get up!
LOVE!!!
Come on man!
From
To. Mr. Ward

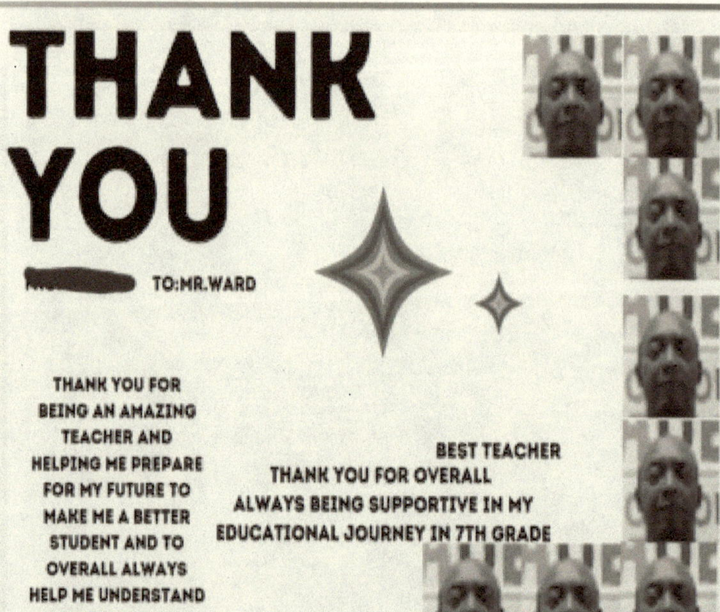
THANK YOU
TO:MR.WARD
THANK YOU FOR BEING AN AMAZING TEACHER AND HELPING ME PREPARE FOR MY FUTURE TO MAKE ME A BETTER STUDENT AND TO OVERALL ALWAYS HELP ME UNDERSTAND EVERYTHING BETTER.
BEST TEACHER
THANK YOU FOR OVERALL ALWAYS BEING SUPPORTIVE IN MY EDUCATIONAL JOURNEY IN 7TH GRADE

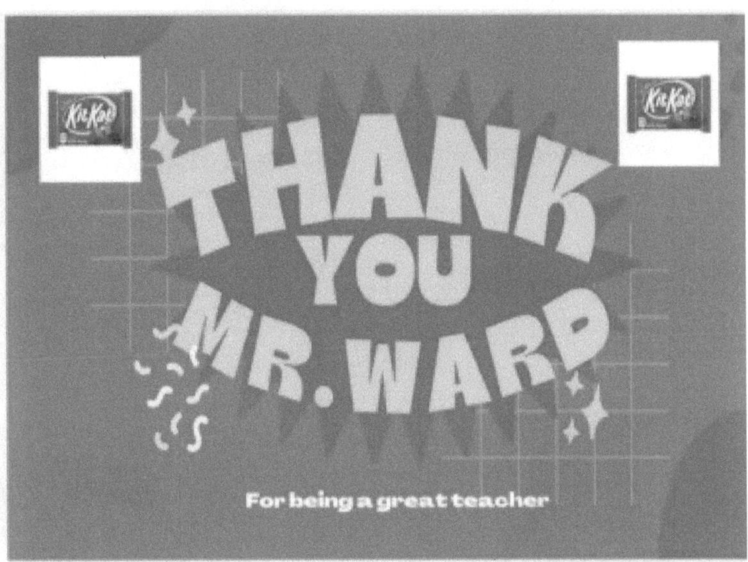
THANK
YOU
MR. WARD
For being a great teacher

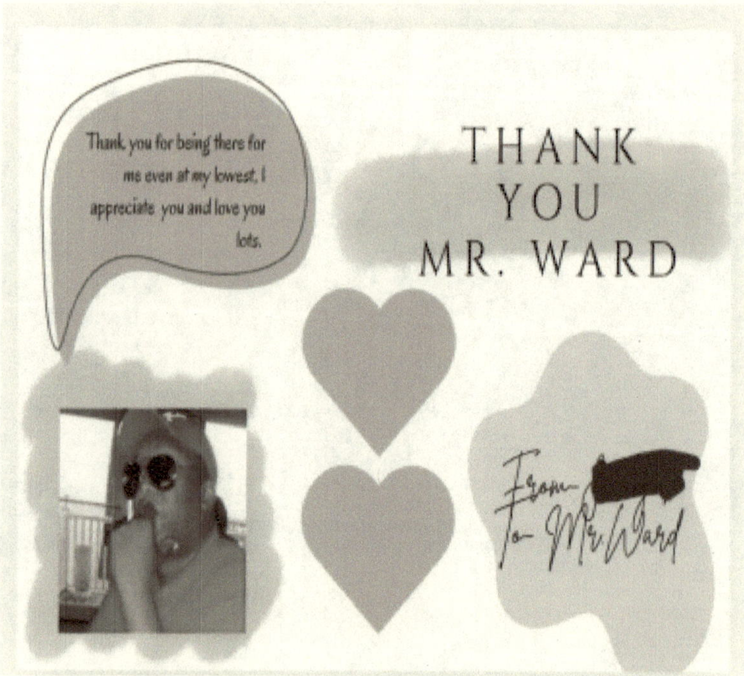
Thank you for being there for me even at my lowest, I appreciate you and love you lots.
THANK YOU MR. WARD
From
To Mr. Ward

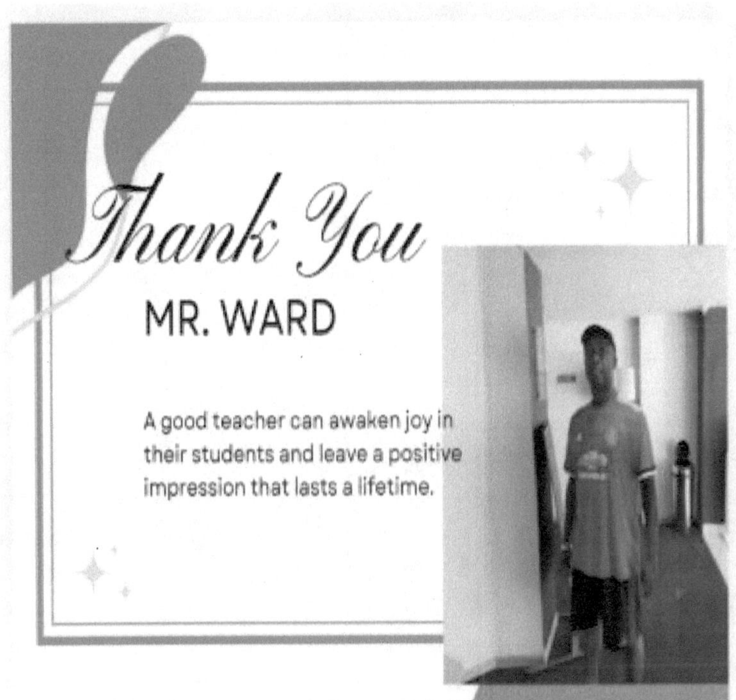
Thank You
MR. WARD
A good teacher can awaken joy in
their students and leave a positive
impression that lasts a lifetime.

going one page

it been going All
right I try helping someone
and they are so rude
it happened today as
well when I messed something
I try helping they say I
dont care I try helping
again and one of them say
shut up I found that
very rude and people in this
School are very rude
only reason my school
hasn't been bad is Mr. ward
How Funny He is and kind
and My Friends if For
them I would have move out
the school so yeah my school
been allright Just people so
rude and was
pretty Nice and only reason
she gets mad because
people act up and been
rude to her thanks For
reading How My school year
been

THANK YOU!
Mr. Ward
thank you for helping me grow
We need S'more teachers like you!
Thank you for BEE-ing an amazing teacher
NO 1 TEACHER
You make a BIG difference
Thank you for being such a good teacher this year & for being a friend to all your students at the same time! -

thank you teacher!

thank you mr. ward for pushing me to do
Better Even when i gave you a hard
time, you have helped me in many ways
your the reason i was albe to get a 3 on
my Ela fast test So i really Appreciate
you what i appreciate Most about you is
that Even tho i yelled at you and talked
Back,
Because of you, i feel like i try hard
engh i can get good grades and
maybe go to College and Live a good
Rich Life
you are the Best teacher I ever had
you pushed Even when I gave up and
Didn't care about my grades
you make our classroom Better Place
Because you push us to Do Better
and to go to College and Live a good
Life not a Broke Life thank you mr. ward.

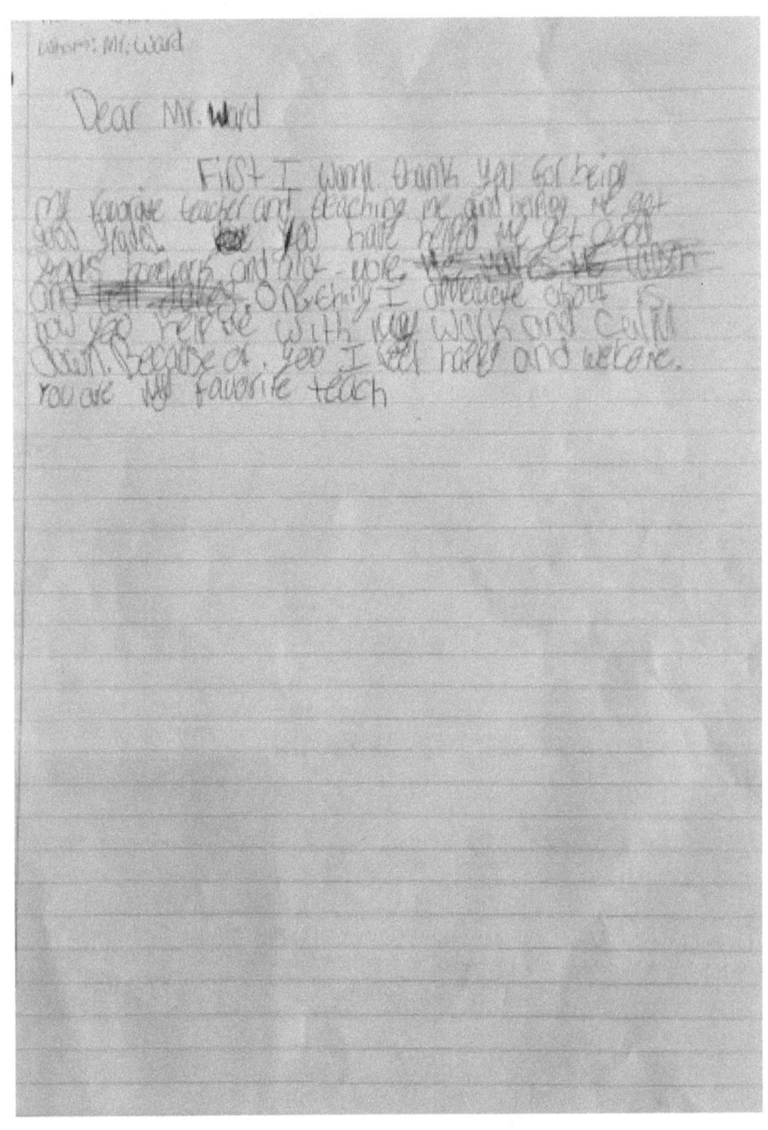

Whom: Mr. Ward

Dear Mr. Ward

First I wanna thank you for being my favorite teacher and teaching me and helping me get good grades. You have helped me get good grades homework and class-work [illegible] and [illegible]. One thing I appreciate about is how you help me with my work and calm down. Because of you I feel happy and welcome. You are my favorite teach

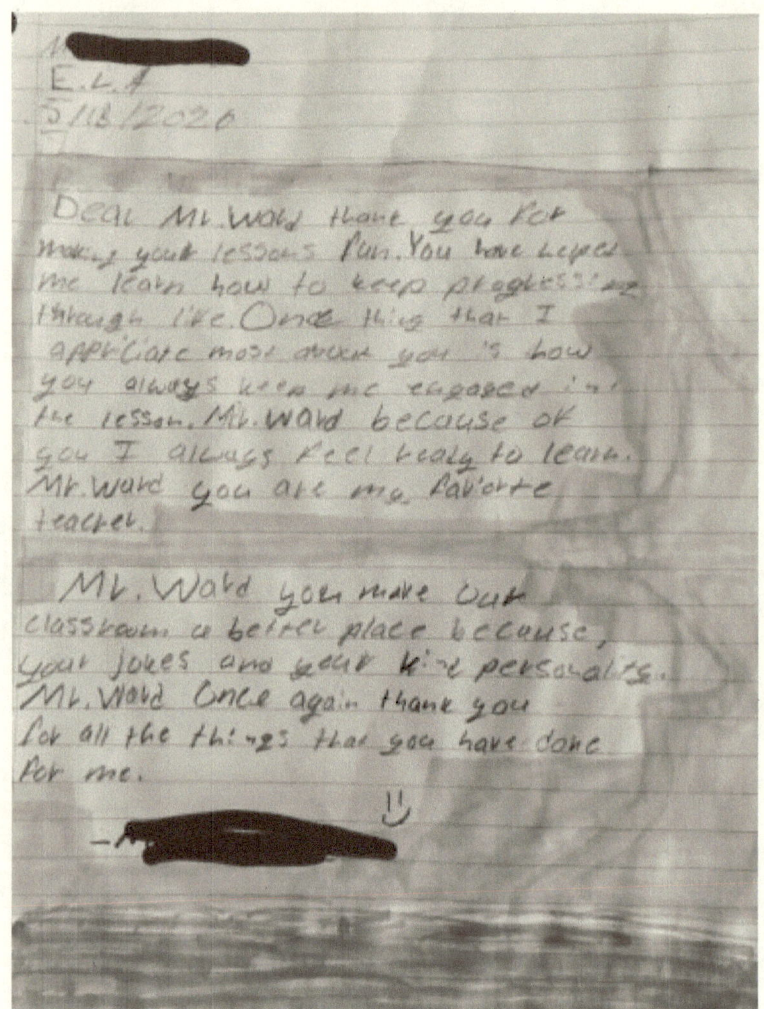

E.L.A
5/18/2020

Dear Mr. Ward thank you for making your lessons fun. You have helped me learn how to keep progressing through life. One thing that I appreciate most about you is how you always keep me engaged in the lesson. Mr. Ward because of you I always feel ready to learn. Mr. Ward you are my favorite teacher.

Mr. Ward you make our classroom a better place because, your jokes and your kind personality. Mr. Ward once again thank you for all the things that you have done for me.

:)

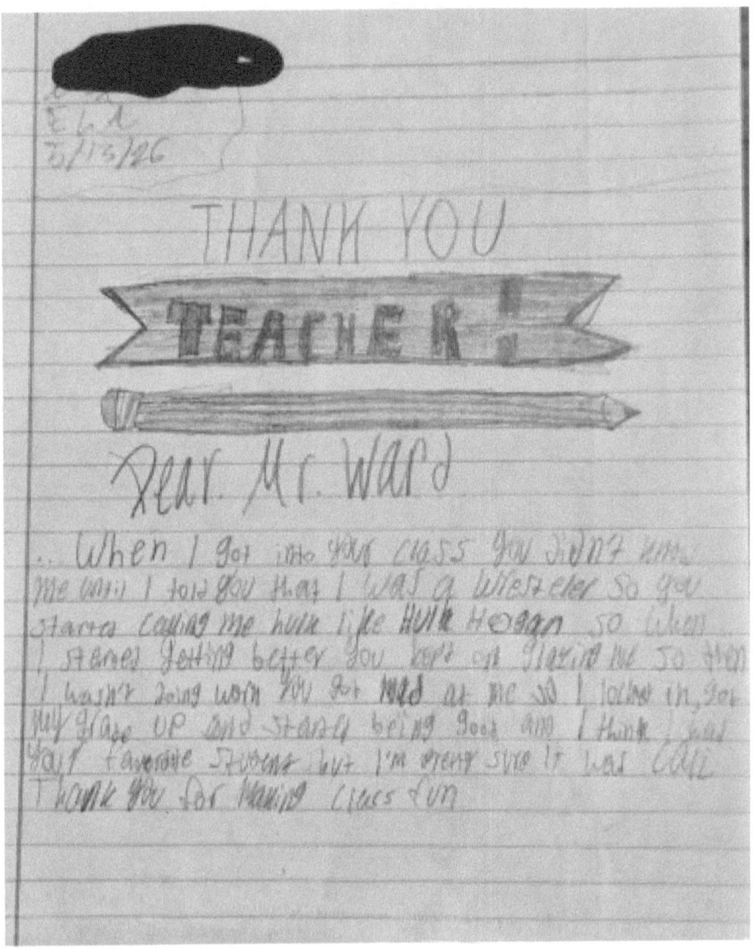

ELA
3/13/26

THANK YOU

TEACHER!

Dear. Mr. Ward

When I got into your class you didn't know me until I told you that I was a wrestler so you started calling me hulk like Hulk Hogan so when I started getting better you kept on [illegible] me so then I wasn't doing work you got mad at me so I locked in, got my grade up and started being good and I think I was your favorite student but I'm pretty sure it was [illegible]
Thank you for making class fun

THANK you

TEACHER

Ms. Ward

Thank you for being a great techer. You have helped me with my work and helped me focus. One thing i appreciate most about you is you make me laugh even when i'm down. Because of you i feel happy and cool. You are my favorit techare. You make our classroom a better place because you make all of us laugh. We love you so much.

I wanted to thank you because I really like AVID because you're the teacher, I enjoy being in your class, because you've helped me to improve my grades because I've been having better grades and now I know how to solve any problems and communicate with others. I hope if I get AVID next year I HOPE (you better be) my teacher. You are the most funniest and sarcastic teacher that I ever had. One thing I appreciate about you is that you're funny and inspiring...

Thank you

Mr. Ward!!

Thank you for being my teacher. You have helped me learn and grow a sense of humor. One thing I appreciate most about you is Peace and love. Because of you I feel happy and safe. You are an awsome teacher and I hope you know you are very loved and respected. You make our classroom a better place because of your amazing personality.

For: Mr. ward

Sincerely

May 13, 2026

To: Mr. Ward 5/13/76

Thank you for helping us get the courage to study and heping us revise our problems together. You have helped me get an A in math and science.

One thing I appreciate most about you is that you tell people their mistakes wich most people don't do.

Because of you I feel more smarter and outgoing in school.

You are a tottaly nice handsome man sir.

You make the classroom a better place because you tell us what to do.

I wanted to thank you because I really like AVID because you're the teacher. I enjoy being in your class because you've helped me to improve my grades because I've been having better grades and now I know how to solve my problems and communicate with others. I hope if I get AVID next year I HOPE (you better be) my teacher. You are the most funniest and sarcastic teacher that I ever had. One thing I appreciate about you is that you're funny and helping...

thank
You,
teacher!

1 thank you for being my teacher mr. [illegible] you are an awesome teacher and i'm greatful for being your student even though we have up's and down's.

2 You have helped me with my work and helped me acheive my goals a lot and helped me get good on my fast reading [illegible]

3 one thing i appreciate most about you is that even though you yell at me you still help me with your funny lectures.

4 because of you, I feel good that you helped me with my goals and even though you make fun of me i appreciate you.

5 You are my teacher i appreciate you a lot because of a lot reasons and you help me with everything that I was stuck on.

6 You make our classroom a better place because you are nice and help us on our reading problems or on reading before and after fast testing.

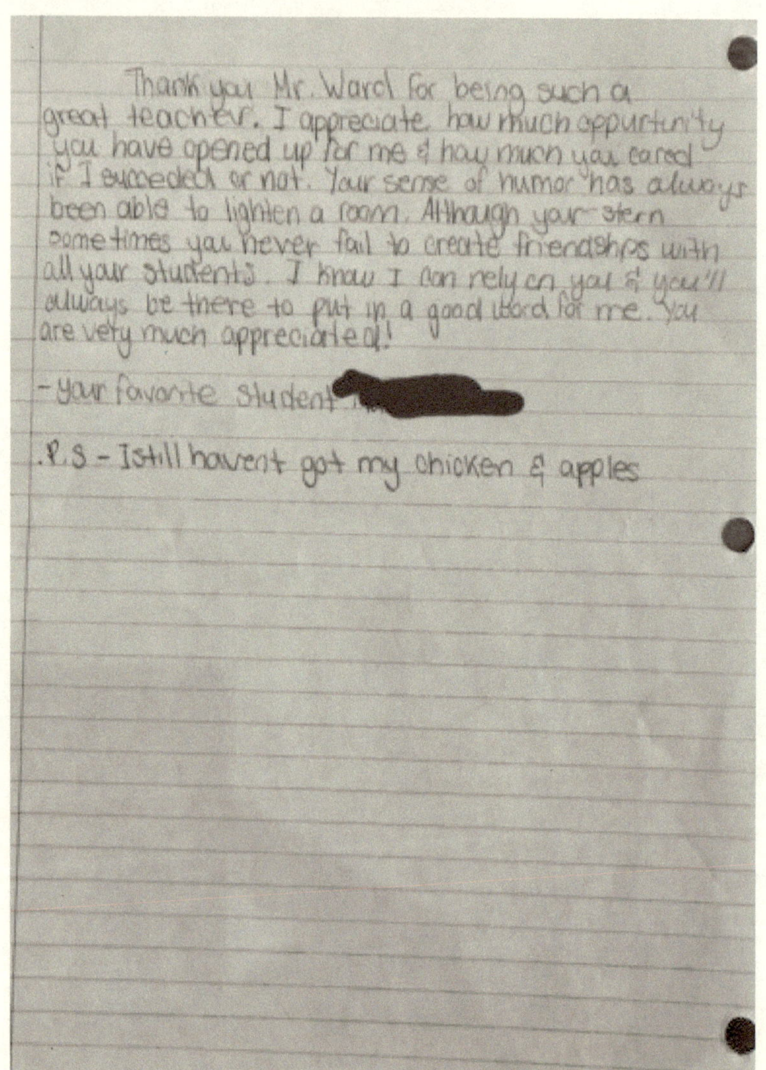

Thank you Mr. Ward for being such a great teacher. I appreciate how much oppurtunity you have opened up for me & how much you cared if I succeeded or not. Your sense of humor has always been able to lighten a room. Although your stern sometimes you never fail to create friendships with all your students. I know I can rely on you & you'll always be there to put in a good word for me. You are very much appreciated!

-your favorite student

P.S - I still havent got my chicken & apples

Thank You, Teach

Dear Mr. Ward...

You a good teach lowk, yo class is cinema fr fr. All luv from here tho.

All jokes aside, your a really good teacher and you've helped me get better and better on my subjects

So, I'm out, deuces.

Peace n' love

Mr. Ward

thank you Mr. Ward for being an awesome Professor. I appreciate your dedication for teaching. You've helped me in 6th grade and now you've helped me in 7th. You make my 1st period the best!

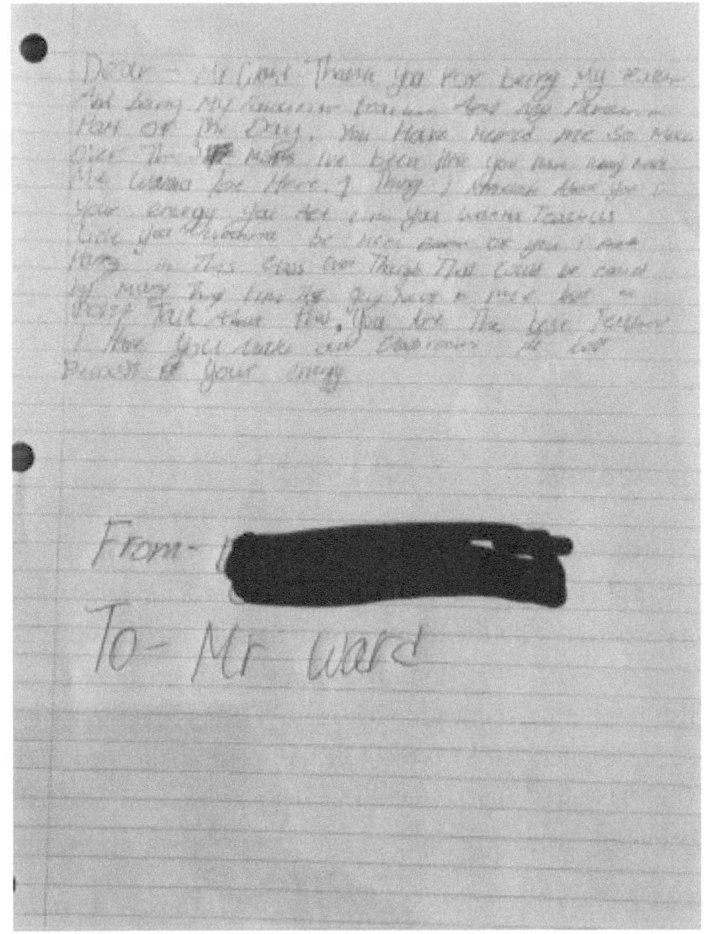

Dear - Mr Ward Thank you for being my [illegible]
and being my [illegible] [illegible] and my [illegible]
part of the day. You have helped me so [illegible]
over the [illegible] months I've been here you have [illegible]
me [illegible] for here. I think I [illegible] about you is
your energy you [illegible] you wanna teach us
like you [illegible] be [illegible] of you I am
happy in this class one thing that could be [illegible]
[illegible]
[illegible] you are the best teacher
I have you [illegible] [illegible]
because of your energy

From-

To- Mr Ward

About the Author

Horatio Ward is a Jamaican-born educator, author, and storyteller based in Florida. With teaching experience spanning Jamaica, England, and the United States, he has dedicated his life to education, literacy, mentorship, and student empowerment.

As an English teacher and educational leader, Ward believes that the classroom should be a place where students feel valued, heard, challenged, and inspired. Through Their Eyes is a celebration of the voices, memories, and reflections of students whose words continue to remind him why teaching matters.

Website: www.wardpublishing.org[1]
Facebook: https://www.facebook.com/wardpublishing
Instagram:https: www.instagram.com/wardpublishing
Tiktok: tiktok.com/@wardpublishing
Email: horatioward@writeme.com
Tel: 1239 989 3348

1. http://www.wardpublishing.org

www.ingramcontent.com/pod-product-compliance
Lightning Source LLC
LaVergne TN
LVHW091813110826
845146LV00006B/1163